MY FIRST BOOK ABOUT

MISSOURI

by Carole Marsh

This activity book has material which correlates with Missouri's Show-Me Standards for Social Studies. At every opportunity, we have tried to relate information to the History and Social Science, English, Science, Math, Civics, Economics, and Computer Technology Show-Me directives. For additional information, go to our websites: **www.missouriexperience.com** or **www.gallopade.com**.

Permission is hereby granted to the individual purchaser or classroom teacher to reproduce materials in this book for non-commercial individual or classroom use only. Reproduction of these materials for an entire school or school system is strictly prohibited.

Gallopade is proud to be a member of these educational organizations and associations:

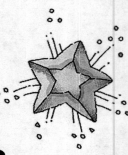

The Missouri Experience Series

The Missouri Experience! Paperback Book

My First Pocket Guide to Missouri!

The Big Missouri Reproducible Activity Book

The Missouri Coloring Book!

My First Book About Missouri!

Missouri "Jography!": A Fun Run Through Our State

Missouri Jeopardy: Answers and Questions About Our State

The Missouri Experience! Sticker Pack

The Missouri Experience! Poster/Map

Discover Missouri CD-ROM

Missouri "GEO" Bingo Game

Missouri "HISTO" Bingo Game

A Word...
From the Author

Do you know when I think children should start learning about their very own state? When they're born! After all, even when you're a little baby, this is your state too! This is where you were born. Even if you move away, this will always be your "home state." And if you were not born here, but moved here—this is still your state as long as you live here.

We know people love their country. Most people are very patriotic. We fly the U.S. flag. We go to Fourth of July parades. But most people also love their state. Our state is like a mini-country to us. We care about its places and people and history and flowers and birds.

As a child, we learn about our little corner of the world. Our room. Our home. Our yard. Our street. Our neighborhood. Our town. Even our county.

But very soon, we realize that we are part of a group of neighbor towns that make up our great state! Our newspaper carries stories about our state. The TV news is about happenings in our state. Our state's sports teams are our favorites. We are proud of our state's main tourist attractions.

From a very young age, we are aware that we are a part of our state. This is where our parents pay taxes and vote and where we go to school. BUT, we usually do not get to study about our state until we are in school for a few years!

So, this book is an introduction to our great state. It's just for you right now. Why wait to learn about your very own state? It's an exciting place and reading about it now will give you a head start for that time when you "officially" study our state history! Enjoy,

Carole Marsh

Missouri
Let's Have Words!

Make as many words as you can from the letters in the words:

MISSOURI,
THE SHOW-ME STATE

_____   _____   _____

_____   _____   _____

_____   _____   _____

_____   _____   _____

_____   _____   _____

_____   _____   _____

_____   _____   _____

_____   _____   _____

_____   _____   _____

_____   _____   _____

Missouri
The 24th State

Do you know when Missouri became a state? Missouri became the 24th state on August 10, 1821.

Color Missouri red. Color the rest of the United States shown here green.

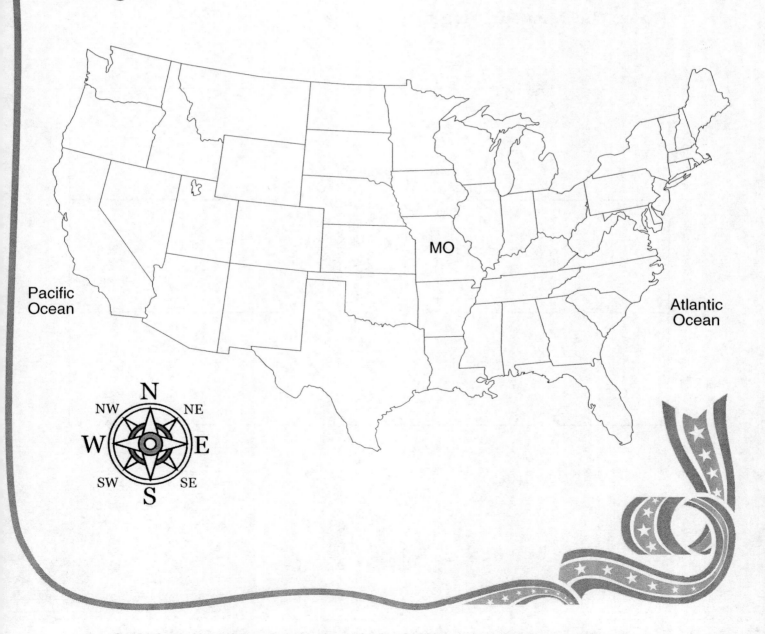

Missouri
State Flag

Do you feel proud when you see the Missouri state flag flying high overhead? The Missouri state flag was adopted in 1913. It has three horizontal stripes of red, white, and blue. A circle of 24 stars surround the state seal.

Color the Missouri flag below.

I pledge allegiance...

Missouri
State Bird

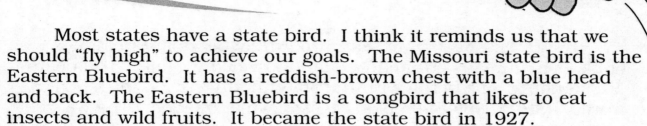

Most states have a state bird. I think it reminds us that we should "fly high" to achieve our goals. The Missouri state bird is the Eastern Bluebird. It has a reddish-brown chest with a blue head and back. The Eastern Bluebird is a songbird that likes to eat insects and wild fruits. It became the state bird in 1927.

Circle your state bird, then color all the birds.

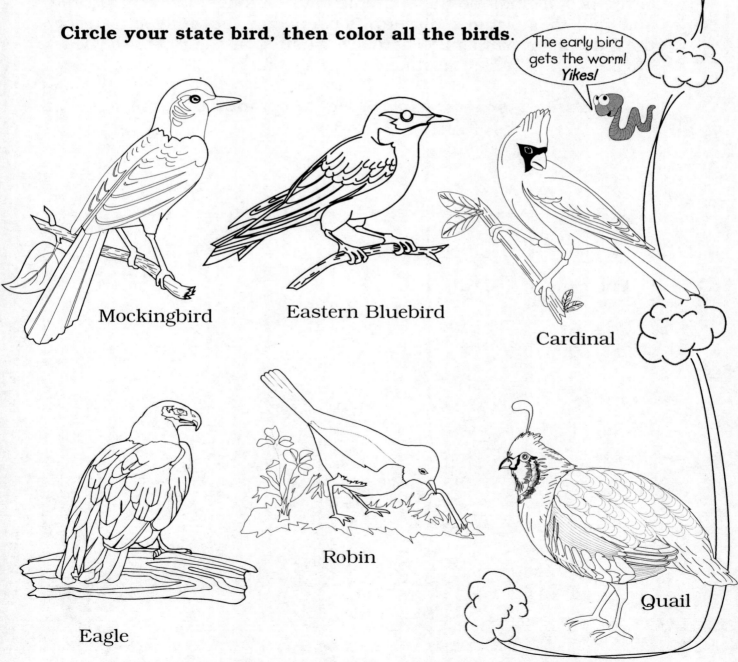

Mockingbird

Eastern Bluebird

Cardinal

The early bird gets the worm! *Yikes!*

Eagle

Robin

Quail

Missouri
State Seal and Motto

In the Missouri state seal, two grizzly bears are holding a circlet which reads "United we stand, divided we fall." The bears are standing on a scroll with the state motto written in the Latin words *Salus Populi Suprema Lex Esto,* which means, "The welfare of the people shall be the supreme law." A shield is in the center and split to show how Missouri is connected, but independent of the federal government. There are 24 stars at the top of the seal. This design became the state seal in January 1822.

In 25 words or less, explain what this motto means:

_____

_____

_____

_____

Color the state seal.

Things are looking good!

Missouri
State Flower

Every state has a favorite flower. The Missouri state flower is the Hawthorne. It is sometimes known as the Red Haw or Wild Haw. It is a member of the rose family. It became the state flower on March 16, 1923.

Color the pictures of our state flower.

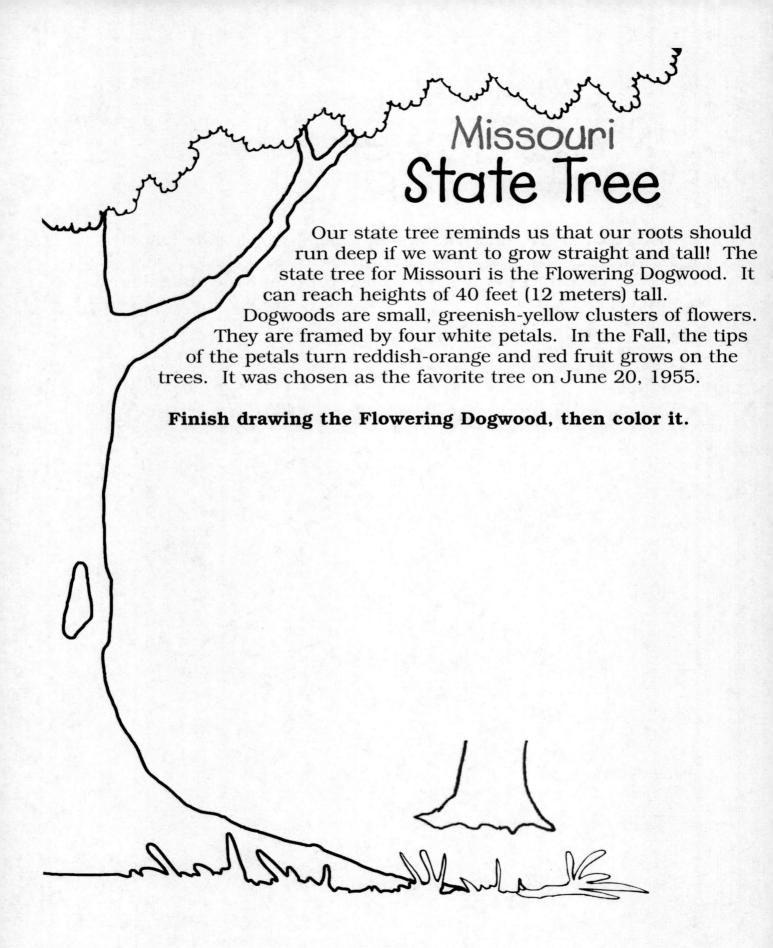

Missouri
State Tree

Our state tree reminds us that our roots should run deep if we want to grow straight and tall! The state tree for Missouri is the Flowering Dogwood. It can reach heights of 40 feet (12 meters) tall. Dogwoods are small, greenish-yellow clusters of flowers. They are framed by four white petals. In the Fall, the tips of the petals turn reddish-orange and red fruit grows on the trees. It was chosen as the favorite tree on June 20, 1955.

Finish drawing the Flowering Dogwood, then color it.

Missouri
State Animal

Did you know that our state has an official state animal? It is the Missouri Mule and it's a crossbreed of a horse and a donkey. It is a sturdy animal that has been used by Missouri people a long time. Our pioneer ancestors used Mules to carry heavy equipment across the Missouri wilderness. Missouri farmers used Mules for many years to help them plow their fields. Even Missouri troops used Mules during World War I and World War II. It became our state animal on May 31, 1995.

Color the picture of our state animal below. Add something to the picture that shows how the Mule was used in Missouri's past.

Missouri
State Explorers

In 1673, French explorers Louis Jolliet and Jacques Marquette came down the Mississippi River to where it met the Missouri River. After their long canoe trip, they turned around and went back to Quebec, Canada. They told stories of giant catfish and new land to be explored.

Color the things an explorer might have used.

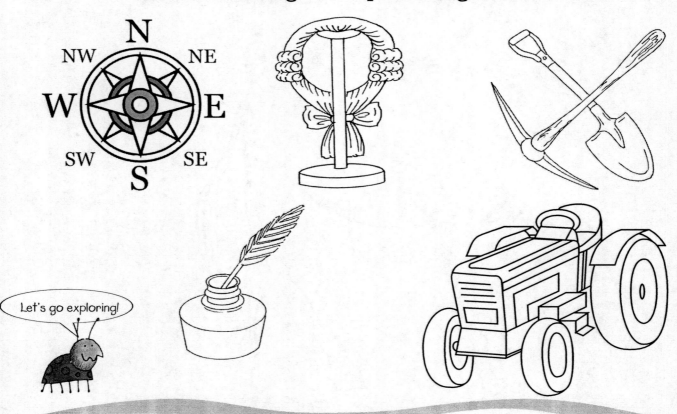

Let's go exploring!

Am I bugging you?

Missouri
State Insect

The state insect for Missouri is the Honeybee. Honeybees are often seen near flowers where they carry pollen from flower to flower. This helps the flowers reproduce. Honeybees use the nectar from flowers to make their honey. They do a special dance to let other bees know where flowers can be found. They live in hives where they store their honey. Honeybees live in families called colonies. In each colony there is a queen that lays the eggs. There are thousands of female worker bees but only a few male bees.

Put an X by the insects that are <u>not</u> Honeybees and then color all the critters!

Missouri
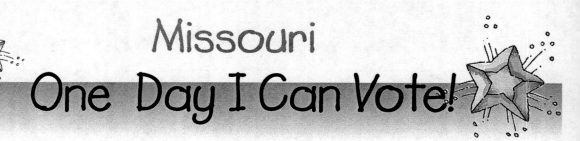
One Day I Can Vote!

When you are 18 and register according to state laws, you can vote! So please do! Your vote counts!

Your friend is running for a class office.

She gets 41 votes!

Here is her opponent!

He gets 16 votes!

ANSWER THE FOLLOWING QUESTIONS:

1. Who won? ❑ your friend ❑ her opponent

2. How many votes were cast altogether? ☐

3. How many votes did the winner win by? ☐

Missouri
State Capital

The state capital of Missouri is Jefferson City. It is sometimes called "Jeff City" by local residents. It became the state capital December 31, 1821.

Add your hometown to the map. Now add other towns you have visited to the map. Don't forget to add the Ozark Mountains.

(CHECK AND SEE IF YOU SPELLED THEM CORRECTLY!)

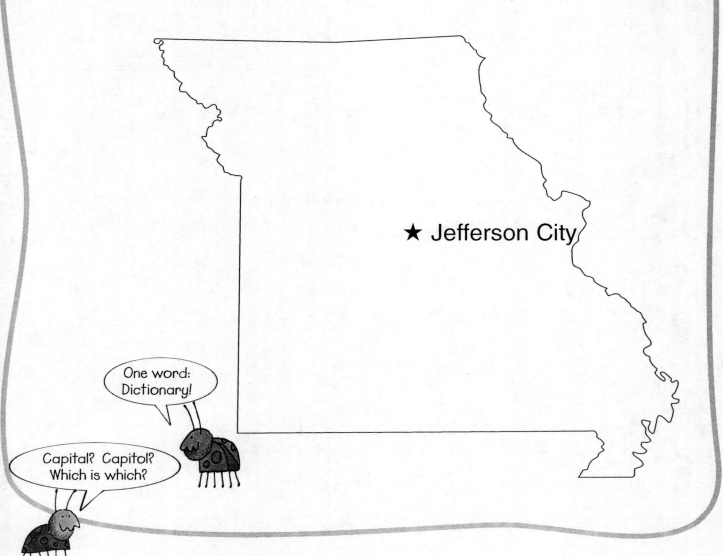

★ Jefferson City

One word: Dictionary!

Capital? Capitol? Which is which?

Missouri
Governor

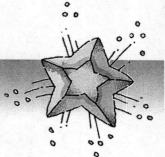

The governor of Missouri is the state's leader.
Do some research to complete the biography of the governor.

Governor's name:
_____

Paste a picture of the governor in the box.

The governor was born in this state:
_____

The governor has been in office since:
_____

Names of the governor's family members:
_____
_____
_____

Interesting facts about the governor:
_____
_____
_____
_____
_____

Missouri
Crops

Some families in Missouri make their living from the land.

Some of Missouri's crops or agricultural products are:

WORD BANK

corn	apples	tomatoes
eggs	cotton	vegetables

UNSCRAMBLE THESE IMPORTANT STATE CROPS

rnco _____

tnootc _____

lpepas _____

sbleevtage _____

gesg _____

ameoostt _____

Missouri State Holidays

These are just some of the holidays that Missouri celebrates.

Number these holidays in order from the beginning of the year.

Columbus Day 2nd Monday in October	Thanksgiving 4th Thursday in November	Presidents' Day 3rd Monday in February
Independence Day July 4	Labor Day first Monday in September	New Year's Day January 1
Memorial Day last Monday in May	Veterans Day November 11	Christmas December 25

Missouri
Nickname

Missouri's nickname is the "Show-Me State." It is called that because we are so sensible that we have to "see" it for ourselves before we believe it!

What other names would suit our state and why?

_____

_____

_____

_____

What nicknames would suit your town or your school?

_____

_____

_____

_____

_____

What's your nickname?

Nick.

Missouri is the 21st largest state in the United States. It is made up of 69,709 square miles (180,546 square kilometers).

Can you answer the following questions?

1. How many states are there in the United States?

   _____

2. This many states are smaller than Missouri:

   _____

3. This many states are larger than Missouri:

   _____

4. One mile = 5,280 ____ ____ ____ ____

   HINT:

5. Draw a picture of a square mile.

Bigfoot was here!

ANSWERS: 1. 50, 2. 29, 3. 20, 4. feet, 5. ☐

Missouri
People

A state is not just towns and mountains and rivers. A state is its people! Some really important people in a state are not always famous. You may know them—they may be your mom, your dad, or your teacher. The average, everyday person is the one who makes the state a good state. How? By working hard, by paying taxes, by voting, and by helping Missouri children grow up to be good state citizens!

Match these Missouri people with their accomplishment.

1. Mark Twain

2. George Washington Carver

3. Harry S. Truman

4. Maya Angelou

5. James Cash Penney

6. Jay Hanna "Dizzy" Dean

7. T.S. Eliot

8. Dred Scott

A. sued for his freedom in 1846

B. humorist and writer of *Tom Sawyer*

C. poet and activist

D. elected U.S. President in 1948

E. merchant who founded popular department store

F. winner of 1948 Nobel Prize for literature

G. famous baseball pitcher

H. born a slave, became a botanist at the Tuskegee Institute

ANSWERS: 1.B 2.H 3.D 4.C 5.E 6.G 7.F 8.A

Missouri
Gazetteer

A gazetteer is a list of places.

Use the word bank to complete the names of some of these famous places in our state:

1. St. Louis ___ ___ ___

2. The ___ ___ ___ ___ Hall of Fame in Kansas City

3. The home of the St. Louis Cardinals, ___ ___ ___ ___ ___ Stadium

4. The ___ ___ ___ ___ ___ ___ ___ building in Jefferson City

5. The St. Louis ___ ___ ___ ___ ___ ___ ___ Center

6. The ___ ___ ___ ___ ___ ___ ___ Memorial in Kansas City

7. ___ ___ ___ ___ ___ ___ ___   ___ ___ ___ ___ ___ ___ City

8. The ___ ___ ___ ___ ___ ___ - ___ ___ ___ ___ ___ ___ Museum of Art

WORD BANK

capitol	Liberty
Science	Jazz
Silver Dollar	Nelson-Atkins
Zoo	Busch

Missouri
Neighbors

No person or state lives alone. You have neighbors where you live. Sometimes they may be right next door. Other times, they may be way down the road. But you live in the same neighborhood and are interested in what goes on there.

You have neighbors at school. The children who sit in front, beside, or behind you are your neighbors. You may share books. You might borrow a pencil. They might ask you to move so they can see the board better.

We have a lot in common with our state neighbors. Some of our land is alike. We share some history. We care about our part of the country. We share borders. Some of our people go there; some of their people come here. Most of the time we get along with our state neighbors. Even when we argue or disagree, it is a good idea for both of us to work it out. After all, states are not like people—they can't move away! No person or state lives alone. You have neighbors where you live. Sometimes they may be right next door. Other times, they may be way down the road. But you live in the same neighborhood and are interested in what goes on there.

Use the color key to color Missouri and its neighbors.

Color Key:

Missouri-yellow
Nebraska-red
Oklahoma-light blue
Arkansas-light green
Tennessee-orange
Illinois-purple
Iowa-pink
Kentucky-dark blue
Kansas-dark green

Missouri Highs and Lows

The highest point in Missouri is Taum Sauk Mountain. Taum Sauk Mountain is 1,772 feet (540 meters) above sea level.

Draw a picture of a family climbing Taum Sauk Mountain.

The lowest point in our state is at the St. Francis River. It is 230 feet (70 meters) above sea level.

Draw a picture of a boating scene on the St. Francis River.

Missouri
Old Man River

Missouri has many great rivers. Rivers give us water for our crops. Rivers are also water "highways." On these water highways travel crops, manufactured goods, people, and many other things—including children in tire tubes!

Here are some of Missouri's most important rivers:

- Grand
- Missouri
- Eleven Point
- Osage
- Black
- Current

Draw a kid "tubing" down the Missouri River!

Missouri
Weather ... Or Not!

What kind of climate does our state have?

- Brisk, chilly winters
- Winter temperatures usually average around 30°F (-1°C).
- Long, warm, humid summers
- Summer temperatures usually average around 78°F (26°C).

You might think adults talk about the weather a lot. But our state's weather is very important to us. Crops need water and sunshine. Weather can affect Missouri industries. Good weather can mean more money for our state. Bad weather can cause problems that cost money.

ACTIVITY: Do you watch the nightly news at your house? If you do, you might see the weather report. Tonight, tune in the weather report. The reporter often talks about our state's regions, cities, towns, and our neighboring states. Watching the weather report is a great way to learn about our state. It also helps you know what to wear to school tomorrow!

What is the weather outside now? Draw a picture.

Missouri
Indian Tribes

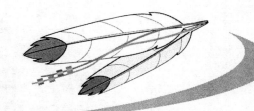

The American Indians were first on our land, long before it was a state. Missouri's main Indian tribes include:

- Osage
- Oto
- Sauk
- Delaware
- Fox
- Missouria
- Shawnee

Help Maize find her way through the maize (corn) field maze to her home!

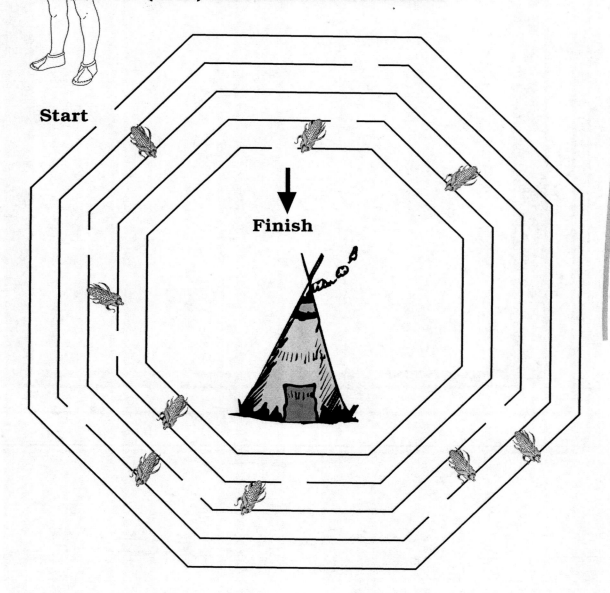

Start

Finish

Missouri
Website Page

Here is a website you can go to and learn more about Missouri:
www.state.mo.us

Design your own state website page on the computer screen below.